In the World He Created
According to His Will

THE

V Q R

POETRY
SERIES

In the World He Created According to His Will

POEMS BY DAVID CAPLAN

The University of Georgia Press
Athens & London

Published by The University of Georgia Press

Athens, Georgia 30602

www.ugapress.org

© 2010 by David Caplan

All rights reserved

Designed by Walton Harris

Set in 10.5/15 Scala

Printed and bound by Thomson-Shore

The paper in this book meets the guidelines for
permanence and durability of the Committee on
Production Guidelines for Book Longevity of the
Council on Library Resources.

Printed in the United States of America

14 13 12 11 10 P 5 4 3 2 1

Library of Congress Cataloging-in-Publication Data

Caplan, David, 1969–
In the world he created according to his will :
poems / by David Caplan.
    p.   cm. — (The VQR poetry series)
ISBN-13: 978-0-8203-3473-8 (pbk. : alk. paper)
ISBN-10: 0-8203-3473-1 (pbk. : alk. paper)
I. Title.
PS3603.A6615 2010
811'.6—dc22   2009026683

British Library Cataloging-in-Publication Data available

This book is for Ana.

Contents

Acknowledgments

Grateful acknowledgment is made to the editors of the following publications, where these poems first appeared, often in different form and occasionally with different titles.

Antioch Review: "For the Washing of Hands"

Blake: An Illustrated Quarterly: "Dante" and "Love Poem with at Least Two Lies," Section I

Grolier Annual: "First Elegy"

New England Review: "Forty Steps in August," Sections I, III, and IV; "Unnumbered Psalm"; and "In the World He Created According to His Will"

Pleiades: A Journal of New Writing: "Of Abraham, Isaac, Jacob"

Puerto del Sol: "The Door"

Seneca Review: "Forty Steps in August," Section II

Virginia Quarterly Review: "Yemin Moshe"; "Holy Sepulchre"; "Beit Midrash"; "On Another Attempt to Blow Up the Dome of the Rock"; "Shacharit"; "Dollars"; "Red Heifer Steakhouse"; "Mandelbaum Gate"; "The Self in Jerusalem"; "The Last Ditch Battle Museum"; *"The Jews have become ordinary . . .";* and "King David Street"

"Beit Midrash" was commissioned by the Eta Chapter of Ohio for its Phi Beta Kappa Poem.

"Whetstone Creek" was written for the occasion of the retirements of Ülle Lewes and Dennis Prindle.

I would like to thank my family for their support; Ted Genoways, who selected this manuscript for publication and carefully edited it; James Longenbach, for his perceptive comments on the poems; and C. Dale Young for his thoughtful suggestions on its arrangement. I am grateful for the support offered by the Lilly-Theological Discernment of Vocation Faculty Fellowship, the Thomas E. Wenzlau Presidential Fellowship, and the Bill and Carol Fox Center for Humanistic Inquiry at Emory University. My thanks also to my colleagues at Ohio Wesleyan University and the Fox Center.

I

Unnumbered Psalm

Surely in some language shaving and loneliness
are homonyms, one sound for the close-mouthed grin
that a razor, fattened with hair, clarifies

and for the inarticulate hiss
of air envying water and water envying air
too intensely not to look back into themselves

and recall when each had been the other.
Together, they silver my reflection and will not clear.
The window opens like December by framing

what's already fallen away, the branches
slimmed to fingers and the mud rooted hard
as a footprint in mud. A boy practices free throws.

Always three quick dribbles, a two breath pause,
then the ball spins into its shadow.
Trust forgiveness enough, it becomes thanksgiving,

a psalmist might have written. I cup in my hands
a hope, clear and restless as water,
for this morning to start more than a month.

Poem Ending with a Line of Testimony

Go witches, a father yells,
but the girls' strides lose their symmetry,
racing this golf course named

for a shipwreck, its low stone wall
where the nineteenth century ended
forty years late, divided into lots.

Sweat bleeds down the singlets,
the witch atop her broom.
Are they better left unremembered,

the Brethren who came here to rebaptize a farmer?
Two failed at martyrdom, let friends pay the fine.
The curse of God or Jesus go with thee,

the Pastor scorned the third.
The Magistrate spat into his hands,
thirty strokes with a three-corded whip.

Crabgrass leans from the wind—
the local histories only it repeats:
You have struck me as with roses.

Tutorial

Before the student

      my mother tutors

            finally understands

how to calculate

      the nonagon's

            exterior angles,

he imagines the pure joy

      of tearing apart

            leaf and stem,

the hosta that came

      from nothing,

            its green tongue

purple

      with rainwater,

            imagines the pleasure

his hands would feel

        pulling down

                the morning glory

that amazes the fence

        by never leaving it,

                its wanderlust fixed

like the math she loves

        because

                there is only

one answer

        and that answer is

                always right.

Last Sighting

So swore John Marston,
"a respectable and credible citizen,"
even if hoteliers printed his testimony
on broadsheets and advertisements.

He saw it rise twice,
not the wake, but the fish itself,
the whole body lifted
from the bay's rocks,

uninterested in the settlers' skiff,
the pistols they lowered.
Coiled there like the town's knowledge
of itself, its sinfulness.

Tide pools thin to nothing.
A boy skims stones where Marston stood.
When his testimony disappeared
into a book, the serpent followed.

Farragut, Sheridan, Grant

When architects laid out these streets,
they knew to name them
for generals and admirals.

In 1890 the town needed the comfort of grand names.

Between Farragut Road and Grant,
on an avenue named for the trees
the developer cleared,
a skateboarder swats whatever he can reach.

Fear is the closest
we get to prophecy,
the riddles and evasions
my brother performed
when asked about the name
they had selected.

So none of us know
if there is a relative or a friend
we should not mention,
a word that carries a meaning
only my brother and his wife understand.

Discretion

Because water works like sunlight,
it finds each abrasion,
no matter how slight,

the small injuries knees confess,
the embarrassment
throats feign.

Careful, she wipes clean
just enough of the mirror
to see her face.

If it sounds good,
the steam hisses, *it is good.*
The good song they hear

is the Reverend Al Green's,
each note held until it gives up its sadness.
Like a god, the saying goes,

and that is why
they should not believe him.
No god needs discretion,

the knowledge of what not to say.

Forty Steps in August

I

Dusk tipping the hill's houses toward the pier
confirms that it's too late for the poetry of light,
long afternoons pretending that no one

has waited here before, that the sand
and the lobster pots are waiting unnamed for us.
And it's too late to be sad about that.

Squirrels leap heroically to the bird feeder;
crows peck out each line of seed.
The time has passed to ask if the cocoon

is the shell or the shell and the worm.
Is it too late except to say *too late* and hear
the two quick syllables gather in the air like rain?

II

Past the usual confusion of light waking in trees
and the bare mattress of fields stripped of hay,
the lane ends at a barn or garage.

There the vintner picks
names ready for stories, oversweet
with vowels, a mouthful of dessert wine.

Freely, we feast on olives
swollen with gin, spiced pears,
strawberries so ripe their skins

stain our fingers,
and Capriccio, bottle after bottle
of last year's Capriccio.

III

No, no one lets their children swim out and see
how small this town is. Perhaps, after lunch,
they'll row no further than the first

red-and-green striped buoy, the island
of seagulls who thieve and curse so gracefully
the chaperon will wonder why this nostalgia of drifting

just past the reasonable returns each summer
dependably as an extra half hour for the ferry,
the traffic of his nephew's questions.

IV

Sundays are for blown-out lamps
and a cracked tea jar in a high-backed chair,
velvet that once knew the elegance of green.

Especially this late, we bargain only with ourselves
over a stranger's clocks and bathrobes
and wedding pictures across blankets on his lawn.

If, as somcone said, the dead are like us,
saying the same things, trying to get it right,
why won't they share more than sadness?

So close to the ocean, we belong to the salt
that lattices our gates and cars
and makes our lungs ache when we leave.

Each bubble in the glass doorknob
we bring home recalls
how easily a life settles where it is turned.

Club Secrets

I

Our routine is inviolate. She sets a timer
by the chair and starts some music.
Crazy, all bass, words I can't make out.

By the second chorus
the timer's ticking throbs inside me.

Most of all her frankness compels me.
Close but never touching,
except her long, red, unbraided hair
that claims my shoulder.

So slowly it withdraws.

I would not put these hands on her —
these old man's hands, these bony, blue-veined fingers
fit only for me.

I feel no shame, I don't know why.
As for regret, I wish there were someone
to confess the unqualified joy
that room brings me, the mirror capturing her back,
her sidelong glance that never looks away.

My children would not understand,
my grandchildren are too young.
When it is time for me to leave, she gives
my cheek the chastest kiss.

II

Look, I said, *your head's bleeding.*
You could tell he didn't believe me, didn't believe
I had won. Still, his hand checked.

All afternoon we threw stones at each other,
little skimmers that spun and whistled.

We took the shortcut through the woods,
handprints opening the tree line.

You can wring a kid's sweater
only so many times. I gave him my undershirt,
held it to his head when he got tired.

His blood turned purple and gummy as paint.
If enough leaves his body, his soul can go
wherever it wants, I remember thinking.

III

None of us cared about the church
until it burned, the white ash sculpted
its walls to columns, brick to marble.

Our nearest wall is a mirror
where Miss Emily leads a couple on stage,
although their leashes never tighten,
except when they raise their heads to bark.

Bored, Marlboro men French-kiss at the bar
where a bottle of Cuervo agrees
salt tastes better when licked from a hand.

The cabdriver turns up the all-Spanish station.
Duerme, duerme, negrito,
he whispers to the window.

Te va a traer rica fruta para ti.
Child, translate those words
into a language I understand.

I need your tongue to tell me
whether fire, by stopping short,
expressed respect or disdain.

Farmers Market

Not a rose, no. Not a laurel vine
climbing the arm cleared of hair's distractions.

His sleeves torn as if he were in mourning,
green ink accents hell's little flames,

barbed wire fastened around the biceps,
the words he chose: THUG LIFE.

A Mennonite girl sells him the day's last bouquet,
twisting and flattering the small dull flowers.

Beauty, masters thought, demanded a copy.
Which is why they trained

apprentices to reproduce the exact shade
a lilac cast, bent toward an overripe cherry,

the worm tearing apart
the peeled, imported lemon, tearing it apart from inside.

Ungrateful heart, timid and compromised,
why do you think you deserve more than this,

more than a weekend's hard noon light, the small happiness
of fruit and flowers, their careful arrangements?

Dante

Here, nothing is unthinkable, with streets
all rightly angled to the avenues
and swept so clean by gasping, humpbacked trucks
he leaves no footprints where he wanders barefoot.

Conspiracies everywhere: cameras perched
atop electric fences, a flashing light
that orders a Chevy to a sudden stop.
A dollar drops into his hand. He mumbles

something faintly—yes, a line of Dante—
a shade recalling an earthly life: *A tragic*
beginning and a comic ending to you.

In the World He Created
According to His Will

for Paul Germain

I

The fishermen return in light so pure
they barely see the bay beneath their dories,
the familiar shimmering where morning burns
to afternoon, spring almost to summer.

So they row by rote toward the spindly-legged pier,
the seawall shading the beach to mud.

You, waking, looking at me as if I too were water.

II

Our pace is too pedestrian to disturb
the seagulls on rails, lording over us.
The sidewalk is an upturned palm, its lifelines
longer than towns.

Waving off my elbow, you tell me
something so softly I cannot hear it
above the low-tide, midsummer whispers
of the surf. So softly, a joke is a story,

a story a question. I wish I knew
how to listen harder, without pity,
not only to you . . .
Your hand grips my arm.

We walk shorter, slower.

III

You're stronger, today.
The staccato mumble of wind-helped rain
that I wake to is you
praying in the next bedroom.

The Lord our God, the Lord is one . . .
What returns you to these words
in the pause between tides, the rising
and falling back not only of water?

Too tired, you quiet.
Past the harbor, trawlers wait
for their nets to fill, the familiar
shallows beneath their lead-ballasted keels

always shifting.

II

Of Abraham, Isaac, Jacob

I

A man pares an apple before memory begins.
Silent, he knows what not to mention:
the letter that didn't arrive, the latest massacre.

Splayed on a saucer, the slices
are tongues spotted with honey.
Is that how English will feel

on her tongue, new words
for *grass, ocean, school?*
Her mother curtsies like a maid

in a play, halfway to the floor.
His chair scrapes closer.
Not her father. Not her apple. Not her knife.

II

Who knew how far he could be heard?

Every few steps the boy stopped.
There was no medicine, no liquor
to quiet him, keep his cough from their throats,
only a handkerchief balled against his mouth.

Impossible to stay clean,
sleeping on needles and dirt.

To leave him seemed worse, less merciful.

His father could not use the knife — it was too real.
So he set it on the stump and tied the noose quickly,
looking over his shoulder, the gray night sky.

She never said what made her go back.
No, there was no cry.

His fists just above the knot,
their son pulled against his weight,
the drop too short to snap his neck.

His windpipe never healed right;
you hear it when he talks.
Call the father God and the knife History.
Or the reverse, if you prefer.

First Elegy

The Door

They scrawled 20
across our front door,
meaning twenty men

could stay the night
or however the hell long
they wanted to.

I was your age,
maybe a little younger.
Mother told me to hide

with the cow.
Still, I could see
girls being dragged up the stairs

and hear the sobs
beneath the men's grunts.
Afterward, I blocked my ears

but still could hear
the girls being thrown out
the upstairs window.

After the men left, for days
the whole house stank
of the onions they ate

to dull their vodka's aftertaste.

Prayer

We bury our dead too quickly
In graves too new for tombstones,

Scooping dirt onto them
With shovels turned upside down

To show our world turned upside down.
We hurry them into the earth,

Keeping the casket closed,
As if we were too busy praying

And had no more to say to them.

The Dead

The dead wash their hands in the basin we left on the porch.
They bring cold cuts and loaves of bread.
They cover your mirrors in white bedsheets.
They tear my mother's lapel.

All night men play cards in the living room, leaving one seat
empty,
And the women brew coffee that's too black to drink.
Falling asleep, I tell one of your stories back to you,
Back to the coat rack stripped of clothes,
Back to your prayer bag embroidered with a braided flame,
Back to the light tearing itself apart in the foyer:

On the ship over,
I slept on my hands
And with my mouth open

So I wouldn't roll over
And start a fight
And so I could catch in my mouth,

The honey that fell
From a cracked jar
In the shelf above us.

A teaspoon or so
Fell every night,
The first sweet thing I tasted.

The Morning after You Died

The morning was confused with sunlight.
Everyone woke early

To closets emptied of shadows,
Houses buried in sunlight,

Roads so wet with mirages
We barely saw the pavement beneath our feet,

The hill descending in front of us,
The harbor swollen with sunlight.

Love Poem with at Least Two Lies

I

January in Florida was barely September,
the rain still falling promptly at four, still leaving
its smell across the screen

where moths and lizards gathered one night,
summoned by candlelight.
A neighbor scatters rock salt; cars idle at the 7-Eleven.

Godforsaken, a visitor mutters, walking across ice.
Love poetry is poetry written by the body,
but who wants to hear the body's complaints,

its disappointments and disapproval, its self-pity?
Better to remember ginkgo leaves,
cruciform shoots entangled

with ovate blossoms, weeping lantana,
and leaves — pinked tipped and purple ringed —
that smelled like opium.

II

Nothing is simple when she brushes her hair.
Steam pulls from the window, maples

from ash; a steeple separates from the brewery.
Who can choose what to see?

She sees a confusion of alleyways, interruptions.
When she pulls back her hair, he follows

the gesture, her neck curving past a freckle.
A painter would reduce it all to a few lines,

an abstraction. He can't.

III

You have to have something almost out of your reach
before you think it's worthwhile,
a shoe-factory machinist told an FWP writer
paid to transcribe life histories.

The Kiwanis, he explained, wouldn't go home
without seeing the ocean, without having
their pictures taken on the rocks in Swampscott.

At the restaurant named for those rocks,
a man recalculates the tip,
his date straightens the scarf
she wears like a necklace.

Desire discovering itself, discovering what it means
to be almost out of reach.

Two Nieces

I

The point is to disturb
as much as possible: the flat gray water,
the usual distribution of air and sky.

A lens recalculates the light,
the niece who asks
if she should call you *Aunt*

waving just before she jumps.
A rock for each corner,
a pitcher atop the tablecloth,

you hold my name an extra half-syllable
as if the wharf were a cliff sketched in pastels.
That winter a trawler spun

past the fort's stone wall, the boatyard
where a crew angles a flatbed.
Each block takes an hour.

The Barnacle empties, the benches.
Force and counterforce,
my niece jackknives the flat gray water.

Squinting up the hill, the driver shifts into gear.

II

If you don't leave Phoenix, why visit the city?
Once the town line renames *Avenida del Yaqui*
Priest Avenue, a truck waters the dirt.

When I close my eyes, you return
to Spanish, a self I hear in cognates.
Your great-uncle ate only salted meats,

always gave away his bread for Easter.
Why, your mother never heard,
because who knows which secrets

to keep, which to ask of the dead?
Converso, you say,
a better word than *marrano*.

Together a pterodactyl
and a tyrannosaurus with our names
canter down your niece's arm.

My Family, 1921 (Lithograph)

A sable cape improves the first version's
      bare shoulder, pearls
lent to the neckline's brocades.
      Gold silk upon velvet.
Added to the hatband, a white plume without end
      bends under its weight.

Started as a newlywed, signed as a widower,
      Rembrandt's last portrait
of his wife remembers her as she wasn't,
      asleep between coughs—
one of the cheap reproductions Bellows
      elaborately framed

beside his work. Greasy and wet,
      the black stones wait
for the etch to settle. Downstairs, what are they singing,
      silly after keeping still?
Soon enough he'd take them to Amsterdam
      to see the brushwork

up close. Then Madrid for Velázquez.
      A few commissions
so they could travel in style, whatever magazine work
      that could be made
out of the black air, greasy and wet.
      Another parlor scene

thrown in batches to the floor—
      he snaps
a cigarette into thirds, to learn patience.

At the Columbus Museum of Art

Art must tell a story.
——GEORGE BELLOWS

Not a square inch hasn't bothered me
to death, he confessed.
Not the white academic vest, the jowls

he smoothed and shaded.
Not the one detail that could be quibbled with,
the black gown worked over too much.

Doctor William Oxley Thompson,
president of the Ohio State University.
A portrait to win commissions.

He scraped off the right ear, the new wet skin,
thickened the bad light, frail and incoherent,
all he would admit of Ohio.

The bad light of the Franklin County Courthouse,
the School for the Deaf, the light
his father built in and called good.

I look upon his ideas with amazement and sorrow.
His character belonged to so remote a past.
So he painted his father

as a ghost, the eyes elsewhere.
Near the university that returned the canvas,
the two portraits share a wall.

Whetstone Creek

A nostalgist fly-fishes the Olentangy,
releasing whatever he catches.
Go to where the city ends and buy—

four decades followed that advice,
past the football stadium, the last gas station,
the four-way stop where a bouquet of lilacs

tethers a heart-shaped balloon,
stiff in cellophane. Again
the line arches over itself, tautens.

The Olentangy, the wrong name restored
to the muddy grass, the silver maples.
Where whetstone sharpened axes,

the creek stipples with light
as if the March snow miles downstream
were returning to the air, returning as light.

Fridays after Five

for Donald Justice

The sins that make us lovely: the innuendo
of tequila, lick of lime and salt, the office
flirtations of vodka and vermouth.

A drink in one hand, a hand in the other,
pairs of coworkers sway until they're almost still,
shy handprints on each woman's back.

Soon a waiter will light each table's candle
so discreetly the green light will tremble in apology.
I miss Miami when I'm away. And I miss it when I'm home.

Sugar Ray

for Robert Flanagan

Only Sugar Ray, you say, could knock a man down
when moving backward. You rock back,
the victor, then the fallen. A story is starting.

A story about how quickness always beats fury
starts with a punch your mother threw,
a graceful uppercut that laid out an uncle.

But what beats quickness? In a softer voice
you remember a favorite student, a champion swimmer,
who drowned and no one knows why.

Your books are boxed and windows left open.
The office wants another cigar but will not get one.
Etta James does not sing; Kid Ory puts down his trombone.

You weren't the department's first choice,
the chair told you. Some thirty years later,
at your retirement dinner you quote your reply,

That's okay. You weren't mine.

Key West Sunset

We missed the sunset but not the martini
named for it, the curved glass
that held dusk's slow dissolution

into the Gulf, the pinks and oranges
bartenders mixed more precisely than painters.
Bars hung the same ads as storefronts.

Because the point was not the product
but its idea, only one model would do.
Boyish in tight boxers, he wore

a grin too large for his face.
And why not? Wherever he looked,
men checked themselves against him.

Almost, one whispered to his reflection,
meaning he was almost as he imagined.
I came here twenty years ago

for a long weekend,
smiled a man hustling carnations.
It's paradise, we agreed,

meaning we had to leave.

For the Washing of Hands

A couple unfolds a blanket, each corner
smoothed in midair, crocus mistaken
for grass, stamen and stem

fat with what comes next.
Careful, the cobblestones are slick.
Although we were hungry and wanted to eat,

the vowels shivered down his wrists
no more quickly, the wedding band
he still wore out of habit or in memory.

Don't repeat the command; enforce it.
A Labrador chases a neighbor's mutt,
gold atop brown, dirt beds.

Then the quiet peeled off the stained glass
and I knew that if I sat down, I'd fall asleep.
Inside, my aunts pretended to say good-bye.

Unsteady as candlelight, he made his way back,
touching each chair as if blessing it.

III

White Stone

for Ana

Yemin Moshe

Garlands of trinitarias shade an artist's studio,
plainer than their synagogue halfway down the hill,
its ceiling painted with stars, a glass chandelier.

They shush each other and laugh.
Brothers who did not die in Turkey died here,
snipers atop the Old City walls testing

the stories British mapmakers imagined.
What kind of world did you expect?
He kisses his hand after shaking his friend's,

their last words in Ladino for the day,
for the neighborhood peace made too dear.
Perfectly angled, a bride lifts her chin.

Montefiore's windmill doesn't work; it never did.
Only for photographs and spice boxes,
silver stuffed with clove and cinnamon,

shaken to hold off the week.

Holy Sepulchre

They lean their crosses against noon's long memory.
Latin hymns, Coptic chants, Greek bells,
even the Muslim key-holder cannot separate each devotion.

Old arguments queue by the empty tomb.
Who replaced a nail? Who cleaned a lintel
without permission? Which shadow regrouted the cracked tile?

In Aramaic such disputations would sound familiar.
Strange as Jews, they follow discredited maps.
Silently a couple kneels on the unswept floor.

Beit Midrash

One room to learn and pray in,
both forms of argument. A sink in the hall,
a wall busy with hats, boys quote sages,

claim and counterclaim sung like riddles.
Impossible to hear a single voice, a conclusion
raised from the tiny print.

A pond a mile from the Atlantic,
last year's neighbors raced miniature yachts,
the cow lily a local watercolorist sketched

barely disturbed. Behind us,
a mudflat shivered into the bay
as if it remembered the island,

remembered what it would not share.
Ana, listen to the noise
the boys make, three languages

forked in one thought: *The timid
cannot learn and the impatient cannot teach.*
Tidewater hurrying across sand,

a catamaran heeled to keep
from toppling, one pontoon
windward in the air, the other

balanced in its reflection.

On Another Attempt to Blow Up
the Dome of the Rock

Three steps backward, three forward.
Bow and ignore whoever bows beside you.
Close your eyes, if you know the words.

The window closed to a car alarm, a stray
crouched beside a dumpster, hissing in heat,
the air that promises no rain from May to September.

Only the schedule of sacrifice remains:
the perfect lambs, the doves,
sprinkled by the altar, the blood that drew Him close.

A tongue retraces a broken tooth.
Speedily in our days: past the stones
paratroopers wept before and kissed,

the hiss of Hebrew everywhere.

Shacharit

The day's first bus circles its congregation:
a pharmacist bent over the counter,
his head on his left arm, a few psalms

behind the owner of the laundromat,
who kisses his prayer book before closing it.
The white stone hardens like light.

Last night pigeons blessed our clothesline;
fireworks ended a wedding.
Was that why you dreamed

of vultures white as stone, brawling for more?
The last day of the month squats on the sill,
the window fan repeating what we do not say:

My God, the soul you gave me is pure.

Dollars

The doorway a soldier runs past hides its address.
A raised finger signals a million; two means two.
This close to the Wall, landlords count in dollars,
a cot in a closet, a sink for a bath.
Two brothers sort a pomegranate's seeds,
one for each commandment
from *I am your God* to *Don't forget*
what Amalek did to you. This close
to the Wall, each step finds a grievance,
each grievance an excuse: stones
cleared of houses, a trash heap's insult.
When the missionary rolled down his window,
they spat on his cross.
I felt, he said, *like my fists were praying.*

Red Heifer Steakhouse

Three students from Baltimore
roll up their white sleeves and cut.
All that exists is the meat in their mouths,

the idea of an after-dinner Dunhill.
As for the waiter, he stacks a tray of glasses,
hoping to get home before his wife falls asleep.

So here goes. Last night on Ben Yehuda,
a heckler asked for you, Rebbe,
asked when you will rise from the dead.

It only takes only a minute, they repeated. *It's not too late.*
Instead of putting on your tefillin,
how about I shave off your beard?

A finger cocked like a pistol, but no one laughed.
So a sabra snaked her hips to the bad time
a drummer kept, a case open for tips.

You are a Jew, you are holy, the boy said
instead of good-bye. How many prayers have I missed,
three times a day for how many years?

Make mine medium rare, the center pink but not bloody.

Mandelbaum Gate

April 1967
For Deborah Lipstadt

In East Jerusalem you learned how to overhear,
donkeys among graves, the letters
you had to walk across,

learned how a half-truth stays
on the tongue. *My parents love the Bible,*
you told the vice counsel who asked about your name.

Jews used to come here
to hatch plans on how to cheat people.
But in 1948 they stopped . . .

Petra could wait. You could not.
At Mandelbaum Gate the border guards agreed
you had guts but no common sense.

The Self in Jerusalem

Your fist against the table,
wine spills like an alphabet.
So lick your fingers and slur

each letter, your hands
on a stranger's shoulders,
a stranger's hands on yours:

> *Great*
> *is your faith. Great is*
> *your faith. Great is your faith.*

Let the self break and dance to the breaking.

The Last Ditch Battle Museum

To humiliate a man so the blood leaves his face
is to kill him. Just look at the faces on the wall.
I'd rather die with two feet than live with one,
a prisoner repeats, ash on his chest, a handkerchief
to cover his face like smoke.
A widower sits cross-legged in the square, squinting.
Twelve generations looted in two hours; no adults look back.
At Zion Gate humiliation breaks into memory.

Past the Israeli flags, the marketplace changes languages,
butchered calves and portraits of Saddam Hussein
displayed like local saints, curved daggers for tourists.
A boy chases a ball kicked from his hand.
He has his pictures too.

The Jews have become ordinary . . .

The Jews have become ordinary. Yes,
ordinary as this city. At Café Hillel,
smokers gossip like smokers

on any sunny patio. A man cools a coffee
with his breath, checking his e-mail,
newspapers from whatever country he left.

Like this city, neither graceful
nor graceless: ordinary as the scooter
parked on the sidewalk, the box

to hold tympanic membrane
at first mistaken for a leaf,
the puzzle of a fingertip,

kneecap, and coccyx, retrieved from a fence.
Ordinary, the psalms
strangers recite for strangers. Ordinary,

the coffee, the gossip, the sudden quiet
the same as anywhere a husband is told:
God heard your prayer. He said no.

Let others debate the afterlife,
the precise geography of souls,
punishments and rewards.

Ordinary, those who dwell in Jerusalem.

King David Street

A breeze quiets King David Street.
The time for prayer has passed.

Last Sabbath our hosts served cashews,
dried apricots, almonds, figs,
nuts whose shells salted our fingers,
cracked open and gutted.

Each taste named its blessing, the formula to give thanks.

See how quickly the window forgets our reflection,
pomegranates chained in silver,
your eyes keeping their expression as they
return to me, a sweetness on my tongue, a foretaste.

3²⁵   Gen 2/15 7b